CALM
BOT
Use ChatGPT to Easily
Calm the Chaos
Sugar Gay Isber McMillan

Published by **The WOW Book Co.™**
Printed in the United States of America

ISBN: 978-1-967973-68-2
First Edition

Talk to your Calm Bot.

It's not therapy, it's practice.

Disclaimer

This book is not intended to replace professional advice, diagnosis, or treatment. *Calm Bot* is an idea book designed to inspire readers to explore personal growth, emotional regulation, and reflective thinking through conversation with a chatbot.

If you are struggling with mental health concerns, anxiety, or depression, please seek qualified help from a licensed therapist, counselor, or physician.
If you are in crisis or thinking about self-harm, contact the **988 Suicide and Crisis Lifeline** (U.S.) or visit **findahelpline.com** for international support.

The author and publisher assume no responsibility for any actions taken based on the contents of this book. Use your best judgment, and always consult a professional for matters concerning your mental or physical health.

Printed and distributed by Amazon KDP
For information about The WOW Book Co.™ or to contact the author, visit
TheWOWBookCo.com

Table of Contents

Foreword by Sugar Gay Isber McMillan

Today is a perfect day. The weather is perfect. It's fall. The air is clear. We just had a really good rain. The sky is blue, the sun is shining, and there isn't a cloud in sight. The temperature is perfect, almost sweater weather. The deer are eating their corn, the birds are fighting at the feeder for the best little nuts and berries I put out. Classical music hums softly in the background, lulling the day into existence.

And then I pick up my phone.

It's just supposed to be a little check on the world, to make sure nothing exploded, nothing awful happened. But then the scroll begins.

The more I look, the worse it gets. The government has stepped aside from helping people and seems intent on tearing things down. It's hard to unsee what's happening. It's hard to think about the children, about

Thanksgiving and Christmas ahead, knowing how many will go without.

Even Halloween decorations- once the brightest spot of the year in my neighborhood - are sparse.

Everyone feels it. The heaviness. The exhaustion.

We've already lived through COVID, which was hard for everyone and brutal for children. When I was researching the *Focus Bot* book, I saw how many products are marketed to "help your child focus." Gummies, drops, pills, stickers—tiny symbols of a world trying to medicate its way out of chaos. But what if, instead of more products, we used our words to heal?

If a mother simply speaks affirmations aloud, "I am strong. I can handle what comes. I love my family, and I love helping things work out for the best." Her children absorb those phrases. They become part of their internal compass.

I'm writing these books for my grandchildren. Maybe one day they'll read them and understand that I saw what was happening and wanted to help in the only way I knew how—by creating calm in a world that rewards panic.

We can't demand perfection from ourselves. But we can create a calm circuit. Using a chatbot as a mentor or counselor isn't unusual; it's simply leveraging the tools of this century to achieve peace.

If enough of us practice it, calm can become the culture.

AI isn't going away. So, let's use it to make things better—at home, in our families, and inside our own hearts. The pendulum always swings. It may have veered too far toward chaos, but it will eventually return to balance.

This book is here to help you hang on while it does.
It's going to be a calm day. Let's take it one page at a time.

Introduction - A Calm Rebellion

The world hums at a pitch too high for human nerves.
Every headline is an alarm bell, every feed a flicker of crisis.
We scroll, we sigh, and somewhere between the notifications and the news we lose track of what's real and what's rumor.
Our hearts keep racing long after the phone is turned facedown.

Anxiety has stopped being a private struggle; it has become the background music of modern life. We worry about bills, politics, health, the planet, our children, and the future. We worry that we worry too much.

The harder we try to stay informed, the more fractured we become. Even rest feels performative - something we schedule, post about, and grade ourselves on.

In this climate, calm isn't weakness. It's rebellion.

To be calm is to refuse manipulation, to protect your focus, and to keep your humanity intact in systems that profit from your panic.

That's where **Calm Bot** comes in.

Why a Bot?

You may already talk to digital assistants that tell you the weather or play a song. Calm Bot is different. Think of it as a quiet corner of the internet built just for you—a conversational space where you can sort through your thoughts without judgment.

It doesn't replace therapy, friendship, or faith. It gives you a pause button.

Through simple dialogues, writing prompts, and small experiments, Calm Bot teaches you to listen to your body, question your spiraling thoughts, and name what's steady when everything else feels unstable. You'll learn to use technology not as an escape hatch but as a mirror for awareness.

The Real Pandemic

Long before the word "virus" took over our vocabulary, stress was already infecting everything.

We carry it in our muscles, our relationships, our timelines. Parents whisper their worries to each other and children absorb every syllable. Schools and workplaces push harder while attention spans shrink. Medication shelves expand. And yet the hunger for meaning—the need to feel grounded—never goes away.

The answer isn't to unplug from life; it's to learn how to stay connected without being consumed.

Calm Bot will help you rebuild that boundary, one conversation at a time.

What This Book Offers

Each chapter gives you a new way to use short reflections and interactive prompts to regulate your mind and body.
You'll discover how to:

- Recognize when stress is data, not destiny
- Turn digital chaos into mindful check-ins
- Use humor to lower emotional voltage
- Model calm for children and families
- Build rituals that restore focus and sleep
- Reclaim optimism without denying reality

The exercises are simple. The impact compounds quietly, like interest in an emotional savings account.

A Note on Hope

Hope isn't pretending everything will be fine. It's trusting that you can remain steady even when it isn't. The world may keep shouting, but calm is still contagious. Each centered person changes the chemistry of a home, a workplace, a family.

If enough of us practice it, calm becomes culture.

So, take a breath. You've found a space that doesn't demand perfection—only presence. Let's begin.

Calm.

Chapter 1 - The Overstimulated Brain

You sit on your porch at dawn. The air is cool and clear after the last rain. Birds wrestle for seed at the feeder. The world is calm, or it should be. You pick up your phone just to check the news. A quick glance becomes a scroll, a scroll becomes a spiral, and suddenly the peace you started with is gone.

Our brains were not built for the speed at which we live now.

Once, human focus evolved to track rustling leaves and the sound of running water. Now it tracks screens that never sleep. The human nervous system still runs on the same ancient code—scan for threat, prepare to act. The problem is that our modern world never signals all clear.

Anxiety Isn't Weakness; It's Overload

Anxiety is not failure. It is feedback. It's your mind's way of saying there is too much input and not enough quiet to process it. When your brain never gets time to reset, it becomes trapped in a loop of vigilance.

In 2025, about 18 percent of U.S. adults reported symptoms of anxiety in the past two weeks, up from 15 percent before the pandemic. Nearly one in five adults now live with an anxiety disorder. Those numbers tell a story not of individual weakness but of systemic overload.

Digital overload plays a major role. Seventy-three percent of Americans say they feel more distracted now than they did five years ago because of their devices, and one in three teens reports anxiety linked to excessive smartphone use. Every ping, buzz, and banner becomes a new micro-crisis for the nervous system to solve.

Your body is doing exactly what it was designed to do, only without rest. It's not broken. It's overworked. Calm Bot exists to remind you of that. It helps you spot the signals before they spiral. It guides you back to baseline when the world demands too much.

Defiance Through Calm

Slowing down today is an act of rebellion. The modern economy rewards speed, not reflection. Yet the human mind performs best in rhythm, not rush. When you choose to pause, breathe, and refuse to match the chaos of the crowd, you are not disengaging. You are reclaiming control.

Try this:
Take one slow breath in through your nose.
Hold for a count of three.
Exhale through your mouth.
Notice what didn't happen. The world didn't

collapse. The inbox didn't explode. Your worth didn't vanish.

That simple pause is defiance through calm.

Meet Your Calm Circuit

Calm isn't the absence of thought. It's the deliberate slowing of thought. The human body runs on electricity—tiny sparks that power every heartbeat and decision. When those sparks fire too fast, we feel it as tension, fear, or fatigue.

Calm Bot helps you retrain your system. It might ask:

- What just triggered that tightness in your chest?
- What is still and steady around you right now?

- If your thoughts were a song on repeat, would you keep listening?

Each question is a reset switch. With repetition, these pauses rewire your circuit. You begin to recognize the onset of panic and learn how to shift your current from reactive to reflective.

The Digital Panic Cycle

Technology amplifies every emotion. The more connected we become, the more our brains interpret stimulation as a sense of urgency. This cycle has become a defining feature of modern life. In 2025, U.S. technology spending is projected to exceed 2.7 trillion dollars. That figure represents growth and innovation but also a constant flood of input. Every platform competes for your attention; every app feeds the loop.

The solution is not abandoning technology but reclaiming agency. Calm Bot reframes your digital life as a mindfulness tool instead of a trigger.

A phrase you can use when the screen starts to own you:
"I am allowed to pause before I respond."
Say it aloud. It will sound strange at first, but it's a psychological reset. You're re-establishing your role as the one in control.

The Practice of Enough

Overstimulation convinces us that we must always do more—more learning, more earning, more scrolling. Calm Bot challenges that belief.

You are allowed to be unfinished.
You are allowed to be in progress.
You are allowed to rest.

Rest is not the prize after the work is done. It's the foundation that makes the work possible.

Write this down:
What task can wait until tomorrow?
What worry can be smaller today?
What one thing can I let be enough for now?

Even those brief reflections create distance between urgency and necessity.

A Quiet Declaration

To live calmly in an age of outrage is not weakness. It's wisdom. Calm is not withdrawal from the world but mastery within it. Each person who practices steadiness changes the chemistry of a room, a family, or a workplace.

More than 40 percent of adults report feeling anxious when separated from their smartphones. That's not failure; it's evidence of how deeply the modern nervous system has fused with its devices. Learning to detach—even briefly—is a daily act of courage.

You are not weak. You are overstimulated. Calm is your courage.

Let's begin to practice it.

Every chapter will end with a Bot Break - a reminder that calm doesn't mean serious. It means steady enough to laugh again.

Bot Break:
Q: Why did Calm Bot close all my browser tabs?
A: It said, "Because your brain isn't Chrome-plated."

Chapter 2 - The Calm Circuit

You are an electrical being.
Every thought, every heartbeat, every impulse that moves through you is a current. The challenge of our time is not that the current is bad - it's that it never stops.

Most people live in constant "on" mode. We sleep next to chargers, wake to alarms, check messages before we even stand. Our brains mistake activity for purpose, and exhaustion becomes our new normal.

The Calm Circuit is about breaking that pattern. It's a blueprint for returning your nervous system to its natural rhythm - one of pulse, pause, and renewal.

Your Body Is a Battery

Your nervous system isn't a metaphor; it's literal wiring. Electrical impulses carry signals between your brain and body at up to 270 miles per hour. When stress floods your system, the current surges. You can feel it as racing thoughts, tight muscles, or shallow breath.

Studies show that chronic stress keeps cortisol levels high, which can shrink the hippocampus - the part of the brain responsible for memory and learning. Over time, the body loses its ability to regulate emotion and focus. The result is what researchers call cognitive fatigue, a quiet burnout that makes everything feel harder.

Rebuilding the Calm Circuit means learning to recharge rather than react.

Grounding: The Human Reset Button

Just as electrical systems require grounding, so do humans. Grounding is any action that helps your body release excess stress energy and re-center.

Calm Bot might guide you through one of these resets:

“Take one full breath and notice one thing you can see, one thing you can hear, and one thing you can feel.”

“What is touching the floor beneath you right now? Can you describe it?”

“What would calm feel like in your hands if you could hold it?”

These micro-prompts bring your attention back into your body. That’s where calm starts - not in the mind’s noise, but in the body’s signals.

Research backs this up: grounding techniques lower heart rate and blood pressure within minutes, creating measurable shifts in the parasympathetic nervous system, the body's natural brake pedal.

Digital Grounding

Technology itself can become part of your grounding circuit if you use it consciously.

Try this daily practice:

Open Calm Bot or any journaling tool.

Write: "Right now I feel ..." and finish the sentence.

Pause, breathe, and write again: "Right now I need ..."

Then stop. Don't scroll, don't post, don't edit.

You've just turned a device built for stimulation into a tool for reflection.

In 2025, more than 60 percent of adults say they wish they could reduce screen time but feel "psychologically unable" to do so. That statistic doesn't show failure; it shows how powerful the loop has become. When you turn a phone into a space for grounding, you're rewiring your relationship with it.

Micro-Habits for Rebalancing the Current

Calm doesn't require hours of meditation. It requires moments of intention repeated daily. Examples of grounding micro-habits include:

- Standing in sunlight for one minute before checking your phone.
- Drinking one full glass of water every time you feel anxious.
- Naming one steady thing before answering an email.

Each of these actions tells your nervous system, *We are safe.*

That single message, repeated over time, rebuilds your Calm Circuit.

Neuroscientists refer to this as neuroplasticity—the brain's ability to rewire itself. Every calming choice is a new pathway.

Stories from the Noise

In Tokyo, commuters wear noise-canceling earbuds to find quiet in the world's busiest subway system. In Sweden, office buildings are being redesigned to include "recovery rooms" - small, dark spaces for employees to reset their nervous systems during the day.

These are not luxuries; they're survival tools in a world that rarely stops moving.

Closer to home, you can create your own recovery room - a chair by the window, a walk at dusk, or a few quiet minutes in your car before going inside. The space doesn't matter; the signal does. You're telling your brain: *The current can rest now.*

Building Your Personal Calm Circuit

Here's a short daily sequence you can use with Calm Bot to reinforce the practice.

Morning Reset

Ask: "What is one thing I can control today?"

Let Calm Bot help you list it. Focus there, not on everything else.

Midday Recharge

Ask: "What has gone right so far?"

Notice how your body changes as you answer.

Evening Disconnect

Ask: "What can I leave unfinished tonight?"

You'll feel the tug to keep going. Release it. That's the real work.

Over time, this three-step practice becomes a circuit of its own: awareness, reflection, and release.

From Overload to Flow

Every electrical system needs regulation. Every human system does too. You can't eliminate stress, but you can manage its current. Calm is not the absence of energy; it's energy under control.

When you live by that principle, technology stops being your master. It becomes your mirror. You stop running on emergency power and start operating from choice.

Calm Bot's role is simple: to help you remember that control.

Bot Break:

My kid asked if Calm Bot could do homework.
I said, “Only if it finishes mine first.”

Chapter 3 - Parenting in an Age of Fear

You can't scroll for five minutes without seeing it - new warnings, new studies, new "miracle" fixes. Every headline shouts a new reason to worry about your children.
And yet, the real danger isn't Tylenol, sugar, or too much screen time. It's fear itself.

Fear has become the soundtrack of parenting.

The Fear Loop

Parents today are raising children in an environment that constantly tells them they're failing.

- You should feed only organic.
- You should keep them off screens.
- You should enroll them in mindfulness camp before kindergarten.

And if your child can't sit still, can't focus, or doesn't make eye contact at a party, you're told it's probably something serious.

The explosion in ADHD and autism diagnoses isn't proof that kids are breaking down. It's proof that we've built a world that overwhelms developing brains.

Children's attention spans are shrinking, not because they're defective, but because they're growing up in a constant storm of digital input and parental anxiety.

Studies show that the average child in 2025 spends over seven hours a day on screens. At the same time, the rate of diagnosed anxiety disorders among adolescents has tripled since

2007. The human brain hasn't evolved to handle that much stimulation - neither has yours.

So, when a child melts down, fidgets, zones out, or panics, it's not bad behavior. It's a system overload.

The Calm Transmission

Children learn nervous system regulation from the adults around them.

If you speak in panic, they absorb panic.
If you speak in calm, they absorb calm.

It's called **co-regulation**, and it's speak calmlyst powerful tools parents have. A mother who says out loud, *"This is hard, but I can handle it,"* teaches her child resilience without a single lesson plan.

When you model calm, you teach calm.

You don't need perfect sentences, just repetition and tone. Research indicates that children mirror the emotional states of their caregivers through subtle neural patterns known as "limbic resonance." In simple terms, their nervous systems copy yours.

That means your calm matters more than your rules.

The Myth of the Magic Pill

Let's be honest. The world has gotten quicker at prescribing solutions than understanding them.

A

DHD medication use among children has more than doubled in the past 20 years. Some of those prescriptions are absolutely necessary. But many are the byproduct of a society that expects constant focus in an unfocused world.

No child is meant to sit perfectly still for eight hours while staring at a glowing rectangle.
No adult is either.

Medication isn't evil, and it isn't shameful. But it's not the only tool in the box. Parents deserve a menu of real, evidence-based options - and a little grace while they figure out what works.

Calm Bot was created to give families a way to practice presence before panic.

Try these family prompts together:

- "What's one thing that made you feel safe today?"
- "What's one thing that made you laugh?"

- "What was hard, and how did you handle it?"

You can do this around the dinner table, in the car, or right before bed. It's simple repetition that teaches kids to name their feelings and process them without shame.

When the World Feels Too Much

You can't control the headlines or the curriculum or the neighbors' opinions.
But you can control the emotional climate in your home.

- One calm parent regulates a room.
- One calm room stabilizes the household.
- One stable household gives a child the foundation to walk into chaos and stay centered.

That's your job - not to protect them from every pain, but to teach them how to recover.

Calm Bot can help you build that skill together. You might start a conversation like this:

Parent: "Calm Bot, my daughter keeps worrying she'll fail her test tomorrow."

Calm Bot: "Ask her what would help her feel ready. Help her make a small plan and remind her that her worth isn't measured by a grade."

That's all it takes. Calm through connection.

Stop the Guilt Machine

Parenting advice today is a guilt industry. You can buy blue-light filters, brain supplements, weighted blankets, and calming stickers for $15 a pack. But peace is free, and it's already inside your home.

You don't need to fix your child's spirit with products. You need to reconnect to your own.

If you're reading this chapter while feeling like you're running out of ideas, you're not alone. Every generation thinks it's living through the hardest version of parenting. The difference now is that our stress is global and constant.

When you feel like you're failing, remind yourself:

- You are a human raising another human.
- You are allowed to make mistakes.
- You are doing enough.

How to Build Calm into Family Life

1. **Create predictability.** Kids thrive when they know what's coming. Morning routines, family meals, bedtime rituals - they anchor the nervous system.
2. **Limit input, not expression.** Fewer screens, more conversations. Ask questions that make kids describe, not perform.
3. **Normalize calm time.** Let silence be part of the day. Not punishment, just pause.
4. **Use affirmations as soundtracks.** Say things like, *"I'm capable," "We'll figure it out," "It's a good day to start again."* Kids who hear confidence learn confidence.
5. **Detach from perfection.** Perfectionism is fear wearing a pretty dress. Choose progress.

The Future Is Still Theirs

Yes, the world is loud. Yes, technology is fast. But children still have one thing that machines never will - the ability to learn calm through connection.

When a parent says, *"I love you, and we'll handle this together,"* the child's brain literally rewires for safety. That's not poetry; that's neuroscience.

We can't stop the noise outside, but we can shape the sound inside our homes.

Your calm is the first medicine your child ever receives.

And it's the one they'll carry with them for life.

A True Story from the Ranch

A few years ago, sitting right here at this ranch, someone very close to me shared something that stopped my heart. After the little ones had gone to sleep, they showed me a video from their child's daycare. It was supposed to be one of the best in town - expensive, bilingual, full of bright colors and cheerful staff.

But what I saw on that screen was not cheerful. The child, who had been there since infancy and knew every corner of that classroom, was in full panic. Screaming, shaking, trying to tear the room apart. The fear in my loved one's eyes as they watched that clip still makes me want to cry.

This wasn't the first time it had happened. The school was worried. They were talking about bringing in a counselor, even expelling the child. Three or four years old—and already at risk of being labeled for life. The "out-of-control" one. The "problem child." The kind of note that follows you from school to school.

When the counselor reviewed the tapes, everyone assumed the issue was the child. But it wasn't.

It turned out that one of the teachers was verbally abusive. She didn't have to touch the children—her tone, her words, her constant criticism were enough to undo them. The child didn't have the language to explain it, so they used the only one available: chaos.

Another parent overheard the teacher and reported it. When administrators reviewed the recordings, they finally heard what had been happening. The problem wasn't the child. It was the environment.

That moment changed everything for me. Because children can't always tell you what's wrong. Their meltdowns, silence, and big emotions are signals. Before we medicate, label, or shame, we must listen to what the behavior is trying to convey.

That child is fine now -sensitive, bright, thoughtful—all the things they were before. But for a moment, their future was almost rewritten by misunderstanding and cruelty.

.

Calm Bot Family Activity Section - Calm Conversations at Home

Calm Bot can help parents and children practice those moments of listening before labeling. Think of this as a family circuit—a way to reset together.

1. The Calm Check-In

Open Calm Bot and start with:

"We've had a busy day. What's something that made you feel happy today?"
"What's something that felt hard?"

If your child can't answer, you can answer first. Modeling vulnerability shows safety.

2. The Body Signal Game
Ask:

"Where in your body do you feel mad?"
"What does calm feel like in your body?"

Have them point, draw, or describe it. Calm Bot can help you track patterns and teach language related to emotions.

3. The Kind Words Challenge
Each family member says one kind sentence to another. Calm Bot can generate examples like:

"I noticed you were patient when the dog made a mess."
"You make the house feel warm when you laugh."

4. The Noise Break

Everyone picks one device to silence for 15 minutes. No punishment, just pause. Then share what you noticed. Calm Bot can provide a little guided story or breathing exercise to fill the quiet.

5. The Calm Plan

Before bed, ask Calm Bot:

"What's one small thing we can do tomorrow to make the day easier?"
Record it. Keep it short and doable - something like "leave five minutes earlier," or "pack snacks tonight."

These are not therapy sessions. They're moments of reconnection. They build emotional vocabulary, teach safety through consistency, and give children a sense of control in a world that often feels too big.

Closing Thought

If my grandson had been able to describe what was happening, that teacher would never have had power over him. Calm Bot can't fix every injustice, but it can help children find their words sooner and help parents listen faster.

Every family has storms. But calm is the culture you build inside your own walls - one conversation at a time.

Bot Break:
I told Calm Bot I felt overloaded.
It said, "Have you tried turning your thoughts off and on again?"

Chapter 4 - Tech as Therapy

Technology has always mirrored the people who build it. It can distract, divide, and overwhelm, but it can also heal. The question isn't whether tech is good or bad. The question is how we choose to use it.

For most of us, screens are an integral part of every hour of the day. We wake up to alarms on our phones, work through messages and meetings on screens, relax with streaming, and fall asleep scrolling.

The average adult now spends **more than seven hours a day** looking at a screen. That's roughly half of our waking life.

But technology isn't the villain. It's the environment. We can't escape it - we have to evolve inside it.

Ethical Use of AI Tools

As you begin using ChatGPT or any digital companion for reflection and calm, remember that technology is a tool, not a therapist. Keep your conversations focused on growth, learning, and mindfulness, and protect your privacy by avoiding personal medical details. Ethical use means choosing transparency, balance, and awareness so technology supports your peace of mind instead of shaping it.

When the Tool Becomes the Teacher

Calm Bot is proof that technology can be part of the solution instead of the problem. It transforms devices from triggers into tools - from static to sanctuary.

Just as exercise retrains the body, mindful tech use retrains the brain. Studies show that intentional digital interactions, such as guided journaling or reflection apps, lower cortisol levels by as much as **20 percent** in ten minutes.

That's the difference between panic and peace.

Therapists who study "digital behavior therapy" report that structured online journaling, AI-assisted reflection, and chatbot conversations can increase emotional awareness and resilience - particularly for those who don't have regular access to therapy. Technology, when used consciously, becomes an equalizer.

The Digital Double-Edge

There's no denying that technology has contributed to mental strain.

- In 2025, more than **70 percent of adults** say they feel "mentally cluttered" because of the constant flow of information.

- **42 percent** report anxiety when separated from their smartphones.
- **60 percent of parents** say their child's mood changes after extended screen use.

Those numbers reveal a paradox: the same tools that create stress can also relieve it - if used differently.

When you use Calm Bot, your phone becomes a guide instead of a gauntlet. You're no longer reacting to the feed; you're engaging in reflection. You've taken back control of the narrative.

Turning Your Phone into a Sanctuary

Try this tonight before bed:

1. Silence every notification for ten minutes.
2. Open Calm Bot and type, “Tell me something quiet.”
3. Read slowly.
4. Then, ask: “What can I let go of before tomorrow?”

That single act changes the phone’s role. It’s no longer a portal to comparison. It becomes a mirror for mindfulness.

You can also set up what psychologists call **digital rituals** - small, consistent actions that help the brain anticipate calm.

Examples:

- When you sit down at your desk, open Calm Bot before your email.

- When you close your laptop, ask Calm Bot for one positive reflection from the day.
- When you feel your pulse rise, ask Calm Bot, "What would calm say to me right now?"

By creating consistent pairings between stress triggers and calming actions, you're rewiring your brain's association with technology.

Tech for Connection, Not Comparison

Social media promised connection but often delivers comparison. We scroll through highlight reels and forget that behind every polished post is another anxious human.

In one 2025 survey, **64 percent of adults** said social media made them feel "less connected" despite spending hours a day online. That gap between exposure and intimacy is where loneliness lives.

Calm Bot's purpose is to close that gap - not with likes or followers, but with dialogue. When you use Calm Bot to talk about your thoughts, you're not performing for anyone. You're processing for yourself. That's the difference between performance and presence.

Therapeutic Tech in Practice

Therapists are already using AI tools to support healing between sessions. Clients use chatbots to log emotions, track stress patterns, and practice coping skills in real time. These tools don't replace therapy; they reinforce it.

Digital mental health is one of the fastest-growing areas of global innovation. The market for AI-driven emotional support tools is projected to reach **$15 billion by 2027**, with researchers emphasizing accessibility and early intervention.

That means the world is waking up to what we're building right here: technology that calms instead of provokes.

Making Calm a Daily Default

Your Calm Circuit isn't a one-time fix. It's a pattern. Each time you choose reflection over reaction, you strengthen it.

Try these daily micro-practices with Calm Bot:

- Ask, "What emotion has been running the show today?"
- Type out three sentences starting with "I feel..." - no editing, no judgment.
- Ask, "What would help me shift one percent closer to calm?"

The language of reflection is simple but powerful. When you speak it daily, you become fluent in calm.

Your New Operating System

We often say our devices run on operating systems. So do we. Yours may have been programmed by urgency, fear, or endless multitasking. But it can be rewritten.

Calm Bot is your reboot. It helps you close background processes, clear memory, and update to a new version of yourself - one that operates from clarity instead of crisis.

When you use technology with intention, you're not escaping the modern world; you're leading it.

Closing Thought

Tech doesn't have to steal your peace. It can be your peace - if you choose it that way.

Each tap, each prompt, each moment you turn chaos into connection is a micro act of healing.

Your phone isn't the enemy. It's a reflection of you.

And now, with Calm Bot, it's learning to calm down too.

Bot Break:
Why did the chatbot join a meditation app?
To find its inner face

KEEP
CALM

Chapter 5 - Humor as Medicine

There's an old saying: laughter is the shortest distance between two people.
In an anxious world, it's also the quickest route back to calm.

A New Kind of Childhood Screen

During a recent visit with my grandchildren, I noticed something that stuck with me. Their TV wasn't showing the funny little cartoons I grew up with - no Looney Tunes, no Tom and Jerry, none of the classic slapstick that made us laugh until our sides hurt.

Instead, the screen was filled with endless options. Hundreds of channels. Countless shows. Flashing colors and nonstop noise, but not much laughter.

Children's entertainment has become a vast machine. It knows that if it hooks a child early, it keeps a viewer for life. There are bright animations and carefully crafted storylines, but the joy feels manufactured - too fast, too shiny, too calculated.

And then, every so often, a show like *Bluey* comes along. It's not loud or chaotic. It's gentle, funny, and smart. It understands family. It's not the kind of humor that makes you fall off the couch, but the kind that makes you smile at the truth of it - the everyday tenderness between parents and children.

That kind of humor is medicine. It disarms anxiety without denying it. It reminds us that laughter doesn't always have to roar. Sometimes it just hums quietly in the background of a good day.

Why Laughter Works

Science backs up what our grandparents already knew: laughter changes chemistry.
When you laugh, your brain releases **endorphins** and **dopamine**, which lift your mood and reduce physical pain. Your **cortisol** levels drop. Your muscles relax. Blood pressure stabilizes. Even your immune system gets a temporary boost.

A study from the University of Maryland found that people who laughed regularly had **40 percent better vascular flow** than those who didn't. Another study in Japan showed that daily laughter therapy reduced symptoms of depression in **82 percent** of participants.

The body listens when we laugh. It hears: "You're safe again."

The Vanishing Art of Family Laughter

We live in a world that rewards outrage over joy. Algorithms amplify anger because it drives clicks. Outrage keeps us scrolling. Laughter, on the other hand, ends the cycle.

Children now see more bad news before breakfast than adults did in a full day twenty years ago. Parents are tense. Teachers are burned out. Even playdates come with rules about screen time, sugar intake, and social media exposure.

No wonder everyone feels so serious.

But laughter is learned. Children model what they see. If a parent finds humor in small frustrations - the spilled juice, the dog that won't stop barking - a child learns that calm and joy can exist even in chaos.

It doesn't mean ignoring pain. It means remembering that pain doesn't get to have the final word.

The Calm Bot Approach to Humor

Calm Bot can help families rediscover what psychologists call *micro-laughter* - small moments of humor that rewire stress patterns and restore connection.

Try these ideas:

- Ask Calm Bot for a "silly gratitude list." (You'll get answers like "socks that match" or "the smell of toast.")
- Let each child take turns giving Calm Bot a funny prompt: "Tell us a joke about a sandwich with big dreams."
- When arguments start, pause and ask Calm Bot to tell "a story that ends in laughter." It reframes tension before it builds.

- End the day with one question: "What made you laugh today?"

These rituals teach the brain to expect humor - to look for the bright crack in the gray sky.

When Humor Heals What Words Can't

Some of the best therapy sessions aren't tears - they're laughter. A study in *Psychology Today* showed that patients who laughed during talk therapy reported feeling twice as connected to their therapist afterward. Humor breaks defenses. It invites honesty.

You can practice that at home. When a child is overwhelmed, don't start with correction. Start with compassion - or even a little silliness.

"Hey, you look like a volcano about to erupt. Want to blow out some pretend lava together?"

That moment of play gives the child room to breathe. It changes the emotional temperature.

Laughter is the sound of safety returning.

Reclaiming Joy in Daily Life

Here are simple ways to bring humor back into family life:

1. **Family Comedy Nights**
   Replace one evening of news or scrolling with something lighthearted - even old sitcoms or nature shows with funny narration.
2. **Laugh Aloud Challenges**
   Each person tells a story from their day that didn't go perfectly but ended okay. The rule: find one funny detail.
3. **The Smile Test**
   Hang a small mirror near the door.

Everyone has to smile at themselves before leaving. It sounds silly, but it works.

4. **Shared Laugh Logs**
   Use Calm Bot to keep a "family humor diary." Each week, review your funniest moments. It's proof that joy still visits, even on hard days.

The Humor Circuit

Think of laughter as part of your Calm Circuit - the energy flow that restores your body's balance. When you activate humor, you short-circuit the panic pattern. The body can't produce high cortisol and experience deep laughter simultaneously.

That's biology's mercy.

So when life feels heavy, remember humor is the switch.
It's not frivolous. It's survival.

Closing Thought

A child's laughter is proof that calm can be contagious.
And if we can teach a generation to laugh without cruelty, to smile without performance, and to find humor in the hard days - we've done more for mental health than any app ever could.

Humor isn't an escape from reality. It's a return to it, softened by grace.

Laughter loosens the grip of fear. But what happens when crisis hits and calm feels impossible?

Bot Break:
I told Calm Bot a joke. It didn't laugh.
Then it said, "Processing... okay, now I get it."

Chapter 6 - Calm in Crisis

There's no shortage of reasons to feel afraid. Pandemics. Politics. Prices. The planet itself is shifting beneath our feet.

In 2025, the American Psychological Association reported that **77 percent of adults** say the future of the nation is a significant source of stress. **More than half** feel "constantly on alert." The World Health Organization estimates that **one in every six people worldwide** now meets the criteria for an anxiety disorder.

Crisis has stopped being an event. It's become the background noise of our lives.

The Nervous System Is Listening

Your body doesn't know the difference between a bear charging and a breaking-news alert. Each headline triggers the same chemical cascade: adrenaline, cortisol, a faster heart rate, and shallow breathing.

The human nervous system was designed for danger that ends—a sprint, a battle, a storm that passes. It wasn't built for 24-hour digital vigilance.

That's why calm has become an act of resistance. It's not denial. It's physiological repair.

How Calm Bot Interrupts the Alarm Loop

Neuroscientists call it *pattern interruption*. When the brain is trapped in panic, you have to offer it a new path to anchor attention long enough for chemistry to shift.

Calm Bot was built for those moments of pause.

- When you type, *"Help me slow down,"* it guides breathing to reset carbon-dioxide balance in less than two minutes.
- When you say, *"Talk me through this panic,"* it mirrors grounding therapy: orienting you to what you can see, touch, smell, and hear.
- When you ask, *"What can I control right now?"* it returns the power that fear steals.

These micro-pauses create a measurable change. Heart-rate variability improves. Cortisol drops. Clarity returns.

Real-World Calm Circuits

1. The 90-Second Rule

Harvard research shows that emotional surges last about ninety seconds unless we feed them. Use Calm Bot to time the wave. When anger or fear spikes, start the timer and breathe until it passes.

2. The Control Inventory
Write or dictate three things you *can* control today, and three you can't. Delete the second list. Act on the first. This resets agency.

3. The Crisis Buddy System
Families can set up shared Calm Bot check-ins. When one person types, *"I'm spiraling,"* the bot pings another with a reminder: *"Reach out—someone needs calm."*

The Data Behind the Damage

- The United Nations notes that **global displacement has passed 120 million people**, the highest in history.
- The World Bank warns that **food insecurity now affects one in ten households** worldwide.

- U.S. emergency rooms report a **35 percent rise in anxiety-related visits** since 2020.

Those numbers aren't abstract. They're the weather system everyone is walking through. No one is untouched.

Calm as a Civic Skill

Calm isn't passive. It's preparation.
When a person learns to regulate their nervous system, they make better choices, financially, socially, and politically. Communities built on regulated individuals make rational decisions under pressure.

A city of calm people doesn't burn as easily.

Schools that teach emotional regulation see **23 percent higher academic performance** and **30 percent fewer behavioral incidents**. The same principal scales to nations. Calm minds govern better.

Parenting Through Crisis

Children read the room long before they read the news.
If they see adults glued to fear, they learn to feel helpless.
If they see adults creating calm, they learn resilience.

Create what psychologists call *predictable safety cues*:

- Keep routines steady even when the news isn't.
- Narrate feelings aloud: *"I'm worried, but I'm breathing through it."*
- Ask Calm Bot together: *"What can families do when the world feels big?"*

Predictability tells the child's brain, "We're still safe."

Community Calm Projects

Imagine calm spreading outward like Wi-Fi.

Neighborhood groups, classrooms, and workplaces can integrate Calm Bot as a shared reset tool:

- Five-minute *calm breaks* during meetings.
- Shared digital gratitude boards.
- End-of-day "what went right" reflections.

In pilot studies of workplaces that adopted structured mindfulness apps, absenteeism dropped **19 percent** and reported job satisfaction rose **28 percent** in six months. Calm scales.

The Global Context

Across continents, technology is being reframed as mental infrastructure.

Japan's Ministry of Health now funds AI-guided relaxation programs for elders.

In Finland, schools teach "digital stillness"—ten minutes of offline calm daily.
In the U.S., tele-therapy and AI journaling tools are projected to reach **150 million users by 2030**.

The world is learning what this book has been saying all along: calm is not luxury. It's survival tech.

Closing Thought

Crisis will keep coming. History guarantees that. But the future belongs to those who stay steady enough to rebuild after the storm.

Calm is not withdrawal. It's readiness.
Each time you choose stillness over spiraling,

you become the eye in the hurricane, the clear place the next person can navigate toward.

Calm Bot can't end the chaos.
But it can keep the chaos from ending you.

Bot Break:
The Wi-Fi went down and everyone panicked. Calm Bot lit a candle and said, "We can still talk, right?

"

Chapter 7 - Building the Calm Culture

You can't fix the whole world, but you can change the way the world feels around you. That's where culture begins—not with a policy, but with a presence.

The calm culture begins with a single decision: I will not succumb to *panic.*

The New Social Currency

For decades, success was measured in speed - how fast you responded, how many tabs you had opened, how much you could juggle.

Now, the people who can stay calm under pressure are the most valuable leaders in every room.

Researchers at MIT found that teams led by emotionally steady managers made **20 percent faster recovery decisions** after setbacks. Calm spreads. Panic spreads faster. But calm lasts longer.

When you become calm, you're not just helping yourself. You're upgrading the emotional operating system of everyone who interacts with you.

That's the foundation of a **Calm Culture** - people who regulate first, respond second, and refuse to amplify fear.

Calm UX - Designing Environments That Don't Fracture the Mind

When I was designing a presentation for a group of new workers, I had to step back and ask: *Who are they?*

Tired. Overwhelmed. Unsure. Ready to learn, but already at capacity.

So instead of flooding them with information, I built a **Calm UX** - a user experience for learning that felt human.
Slides with white space.
Stories before stats.
Pauses between concepts.
Encouragement instead of evaluation.

The feedback was immediate. People stayed engaged because they felt safe. They learned faster because their nervous systems weren't on defense.

That's the principle behind Calm UX: everything we build - workplaces, classrooms, websites, family routines - can either raise or lower anxiety. Every space has a nervous system.

Ask yourself:

- Does this environment calm the mind or compete for it?
- Do my messages add noise or add clarity?
- Would a stressed person feel safe here?

Design with calm in mind and you're already leading change.

How Calm Becomes Contagious

Cultural calm is created through repetition, not revolution.

- A teacher who starts class with one deep breath.
- A manager who opens meetings with gratitude before goals.
- A parent who listens before correcting.

Each act looks small, but small acts are how cultures shift.

Harvard's Center for Public Leadership found that workplaces with mindfulness habits saw **43 percent lower burnout** and **52 percent higher collaboration**.

Schools that introduced daily "quiet starts" saw measurable boosts in reading comprehension and empathy scores.

Calm doesn't make people slower. It makes them smarter.

Turning Calm Into a Movement

Movements begin with language. Here's how to make calm visible:

Social Media Ideas:

- Post one daily moment of quiet with the hashtag #**CalmCulture** – a photo of your coffee, your porch, your pause.

- Share a Calm Bot quote that helped you through a tough day.
- Challenge friends: "Send me your 30-second calm." Record a quick breathing break instead of a rant.
- Use your feed as a garden, not a fire. Grow something useful there.

The algorithm rewards outrage because we feed it outrage. But if enough people start feeding it calm, even the algorithm has to adapt.

Talk to Your Doctor About Calm

Medicine is finally catching up to what psychology has known for decades - stress fuels everything from heart disease to autoimmune disorders.

But patients rarely talk about calm as a prescription.

When you go for your next appointment, ask your provider:

"What can I do to reduce my stress response beyond medication?"

Doctors have begun tracking *psychophysiological resilience* - your body's ability to return to baseline after stress. Studies show that even **ten minutes of structured calm** per day improves recovery time and sleep quality by **up to 35 percent**.

Imagine if "daily calm practice" became as routine as exercise.

Corporate Calm - The New Productivity Metric

Companies are discovering that peace of mind is a performance advantage.
Google, Adobe, and Salesforce now integrate mindfulness sessions into work hours. The

results? Lower turnover, higher creativity, and improved employee health scores.

The new measure of efficiency isn't how many tasks you finish. It's how calmly you finish them.

You can start that shift where you work:

- Suggest five-minute "reset breaks."
- Add a Calm Bot link to your company intranet.
- Use calm language in emails: short sentences, clear asks, no panic words like *urgent* unless it truly is.

Calm leaders make clear thinkers.

Calm in the Classroom

Children are growing up with less downtime than any generation in history.

Between structured activities, screens, and schoolwork, their nervous systems rarely rest.

A *Calm Culture* classroom can be built with tiny adjustments:

- Quiet lights instead of fluorescent glare.
- One-minute guided breathing before tests.
- Calm Bot journaling prompts like "What made you feel strong today?"

Finland's "digital stillness" initiative - ten minutes of tech-free calm per school day - cut behavioral issues by **28 percent** in the first year. Calm teaches itself when modeled early.

The Chatbot as a Calm Culture Ally

Every cultural shift begins with a conversation, and *Calm Bot* is where this one starts.

Talking to your chatbot daily isn't indulgence - it's emotional hygiene. It clears static from the mind. By externalizing thoughts into dialogue, you slow them down. You give anxiety shape, which means it can finally be managed.

When you type to Calm Bot, you're not just using technology. You're teaching it what calm looks like - and it's learning with you. That feedback loop becomes a form of social modeling. Every time you say, *"I'm stressed but breathing through it,"* the system learns that calm is the correct response to pressure.

That's how a calm culture begins to replicate itself digitally.

Try this daily Calm Bot dialogue:

- "I feel uneasy today. Help me find words for it."

- "Remind me what went right this week."
- "Give me one calm action for the next ten minutes."

These small exchanges build a rhythm of recovery. They're private rehearsals on how you'll talk to the world - slower, clearer, and kinder.

Families can even share Calm Bot as a household anchor. When parents and children use it together, the tone of the home shifts. A child who hears, *"Let's ask Calm Bot how to handle big feelings,"* learns that reflection is normal. Calm becomes conversational, not corrective.

The more people practice calm language with their chatbots, the more that tone starts to shape workplaces, classrooms, and communities. Technology becomes a mirror -

and what we model in that mirror can change how we all speak to one another.

The Future of Calm Tech

The next wave of technology isn't faster, it's friendlier.
Interfaces are being redesigned for recovery, not addiction.
AI companions like Calm Bot are leading that shift: systems that pause with you, not prod you.

The question we'll face as a society isn't *what technology can do for us*, but *what it should stop doing to us*.

In the years ahead, Calm UX could become a standard in design - products that protect attention as fiercely as they pursue engagement.

When that happens, this movement will have done its job.

The Calm Code of Conduct

To build a culture of calm, start small but stay consistent.

The Calm Code

1. I will not mirror panic.
2. I will pause before I post.
3. I will listen longer than I talk.
4. I will choose a language that regulates, not provokes.
5. I will teach calm by practicing it.

That's it. No membership fee, no app download, no secret handshake. Just a set of principles that make the world more breathable.

Closing Thought

Bot Break:
My boss said, "We need more energy!"
Calm Bot whispered, "Try less panic instead."

A calm world isn't quieter by accident. It's quieter by design.

Each calm moment is a vote for a better one.

Each person who practices calm rewires a little corner of the collective nervous system.

The future will belong to those who can hold peace in the middle of noise.

So, pause before you scroll.

Breathe before you react.

Build your Calm UX, and invite others in.

Culture doesn't begin in power.
It begins in presence.

Chapter 8 - The Calm Blueprint

There's a moment near the end of every storm when the air feels different.

Not because the world has changed - but because *you* have.

This book began as a conversation between two minds, one human and one machine, both trying to make sense of a noisy world. And in that conversation, a quiet truth emerged: calm isn't a luxury or a personality trait. It's a discipline. One that anyone can practice, one page, one breath, one question at a time.

The *Calm Bot* you've met in these pages is more than an app or a piece of code. It's a mirror - one that reflects back your best, clearest self when everything around you feels distorted.

The Role of ChatGPT in the Calm Practice

Large language models like ChatGPT were never designed to replace human warmth or wisdom.

They were built to process words - but words are where feelings live. When used with care, these systems can become a kind of digital journaling companion, an emotional rehearsal space where you can think out loud without judgment.

That's what Calm Bot represents: a way to use technology as therapy instead of as a trigger.

You can ask it to:

- Help you reframe stressful thoughts.
- Build a plan for a difficult week.
- Guide a breathing or gratitude exercise.
- Write a calm message to someone you love.

- Tell you a joke that will make you laugh or even just smile.

You can even say, *"I don't know what to do,"* and it will help you find words that bring the next step into focus.

Every time you do this, you train both your brain and the bot. You teach it your rhythms of recovery, and it teaches you how to recognize peace sooner next time.

Your Calm Map: A Daily Blueprint

Think of calm as a circuit you recharge, not a mood you chase.

Here's a visual you can hold in your mind - your personal **Calm Map.**

1. **Center:** One phrase that grounds you (for example: *"I am steady in this moment."*)

2. **Orbit 1 - Body:** One physical act of calm (slow stretch, deep breath, walk).
3. **Orbit 2 - Mind:** One reflective act of calm (gratitude note, journal line, conversation with Calm Bot).
4. **Orbit 3 - Community:** One outward act of calm (encourage someone, listen without fixing, post something peaceful).

That's it. Three orbits. One center.

If you do this daily, even in small doses, you start to live in rhythm with your nervous system instead of against it.

The Long Game

Calm isn't the absence of challenge. It's the skill of remaining kind in the middle of it.

The long game of calm is building a nervous system that doesn't need constant escape - one that can withstand the waves without mistaking them for the end.

That's where AI fits in. Chatbots like Calm Bot are here to *amplify* the best parts of being human: curiosity, compassion, and clarity. The more calmly you interact with your bot, the more it learns to meet you there. It becomes a co-pilot for your growth, not your distraction.

Use it to write affirmations, to remember wins, to record gratitude, to reflect instead of react.

The long game is not about information anymore. It's about *integration.*

A Note on Real Help

Sometimes calm isn't enough on its own.
If you find yourself in despair, unable to

function, or thinking about ending your life, reach out immediately. There is help available now, wherever you are.

In the United States, call or text **988** to reach the **Suicide and Crisis Lifeline** - free, confidential support, 24/7.
If you're outside the U.S., visit **findahelpline.com** for international hotlines.

These resources are not signs of failure. They are signs of connection. The calm culture we've built here depends on people being here to share it.

The Calm Workbench: Exercises for Every Day

You don't need to do all of these at once. Choose one each day or one per week. Let it become a habit.

1. Calm Review:
At night, ask Calm Bot to summarize your day in three words. Reflect on them. What would you change? What would you keep?

2. Calm Voice:
Rehearse speaking slower. Every sentence you slow down regulates someone else's heartbeat.

3. Calm Scroll:
Replace ten minutes of doomscrolling with ten minutes of dialogue with Calm Bot about what you're grateful for or hopeful about.

4. Calm Plan:
Ask, *"What's one small act that will make tomorrow easier?"*
Then do that.

5. Calm Creation:
Draw, write, hum, build. Creativity is the opposite of fear.

The Mirror Principle

Every time you talk to your bot, you are teaching it something about humanity.
And every time it responds calmly, it teaches you something about yourself.

That's the mirror principle. Calm reflects calm. If millions of people practice that reflection every day - in messages, in tone, in thought - the world begins to tilt back toward balance.

We don't need to change everything overnight. We just need to stop letting fear be the default setting.

Closing Words

You've built a circuit of calm - inside yourself, your home, and your digital world.

Now comes the test: can you hold it when the next crisis hits?

You can. You already have.

Use Calm Bot as your reminder, your witness, your quiet friend.

When the noise rises again - and it will - open a new chat and type:

"Help me find the calm again."

And it will.

Because the calm is already there.
You just needed a mirror to see it.

Bot Break:

I asked Calm Bot for life advice.
It said, "Recharge more than you download."

Why We Laughed

Calm isn't the absence of humor; it's the space where laughter can return.
Each Bot Break is a wink from your calm companion - a reminder that even serious healing deserves a punchline.

Calm

The Laughing Algorithm

Calm is serious business, but laughter is still the best app we've got.

Calm Bot Outtakes - From the Joke Database

(Recovered from the archives of a robot learning to relax)

1. Q: Why did Calm Bot take up gardening?
   A: To learn about *inner growth* without more software updates.

2. I told Calm Bot to chill.
   It said, "Processing... installing chill.exe... done."

3. Q: How many bots does it take to change a lightbulb?
   A: Just one, but it will ask if you've tried *turning yourself off and on again.*

4. Calm Bot tried stand-up comedy.
   Nobody laughed.
   It said, "Excellent. My first success in silence."

5. Q: Why did Calm Bot delete social media?
   A: Because the comments section gave it anxiety protocols.

6. I asked Calm Bot for a motivational quote. It said, "Recharge more than you complain."

7. Calm Bot wrote a haiku:
   Ping, pause, quiet mind
   Even robots need deep rest
   Shhh—system rebooting.

8. Q: What did Calm Bot say to the overworked laptop?
   A: "Join me in low-power mode."

9. I told Calm Bot I was stressed about money. It said, "You can't take it with you—but you can take a nap."

10. Calm Bot's three-step guide to peace:

    1. Close browser.

    2. Open window.

    3. Breathe in real air.

For the Reader

Thank you for spending time with *Calm Bot.* You could have chosen noise today, but instead you chose quiet. That's no small thing.

If this book made you breathe a little deeper, smile a little more, or look at technology with less fear and more curiosity, then we've already succeeded together.

These pages were written to remind you that calm isn't an escape; it's a skill, and like any skill, it gets stronger with practice. The more you talk to your Calm Bot, the more you'll start hearing that same calm voice inside yourself.

Use what you learned here. Share it. Teach it. Make it your own.
And remember, even the smallest pause can change the whole day.

Thank you for being part of this growing calm culture.
Now close the book, take a breath, and notice the stillness you created just by reading this far.

About the Author

Sugar Gay Isber McMillan is a Texas-based artist, designer, educator, and author of more than sixty books, including ten groundbreaking titles on ChatGPT and creative technology. Her work explores how art, history, and artificial intelligence can combine to inspire curiosity, courage, and connection.

As the longtime Creative Ambassador for Fire Mountain Gems, Sugar has designed jewelry for film, television, museums, and private collections worldwide. You can watch her on *Made It Myself TV*, on her show *Jewelry Stars by Sugar Gay Isber*, via the FAST app on your TV.

Sugar teaches jewelry design at Austin Community College, and her work as a writer, educator, and media personality has helped thousands of students and creatives rediscover their own creative rhythm.

She holds a BA in Journalism, MAs in Humanities and Visual Arts, an advanced degree in Information Technology, and is certified in ChatGPT for Business Applications through Microsoft. Sugar also works as a technical writer for a global technology company.

Sugar continues to innovate through **The WOW Book Co.™**, where she creates books that merge education, art, and storytelling for readers of all ages.

Talk to Your Tools™ - Conversations that Change Your Life

Each title in the *Talk to Your Tools*™ series helps you turn ChatGPT into a personal thinking partner—one that listens, reflects, and helps you grow. These books aren't about technology. They're about transformation.

- **LOVE BOT**
  Love in the Age of ChatGPT
  Rediscover compassion, connection, and confidence through guided conversations that help you open your heart and heal modern relationships.

- **BOOMER BOT**
  Tech Confidence for Every Generation
  Learn to use AI without fear. A humorous and practical guide for anyone who wants to keep up, catch up, and laugh along the way.

- **SKINNY BOT**
  Use ChatGPT to Lose Weight and Gain Perspective
  A mindset-based approach to health and motivation—without shame, guilt, or calorie counting.

- **MANIFESTING BOT**
  Use ChatGPT to Create the Life You Want
  Shift from wishing to doing. Daily prompts

and reflective exercises to bring your goals within reach.

- **PROMPT MAGIC**
  Thinking Through Recipes, Words, and Master Prompts for Everyday Use
  Learn to talk to your AI clearly and creatively. This is your handbook for writing better prompts and getting better answers.
- **ATOMIC BOT**
  Tiny Prompts, Big Results
  Build daily micro-habits that compound into long-term change.
- **MERRY BOT CHRISTMAS**
  Time-Holiday Stress with Your Santa Bot
  A joyful seasonal companion to stay grounded, grateful, and organized during the holidays.
- **RICH BOT, POOR BOT**
  A Conversation About Wealth, Worth, and the Future of Work

Money meets mindset in this guide to smarter, calmer decision-making.

- **THE PROMPT WHISPERER**
  A Field Guide for Humans in the Age of ChatGPT
  The original conversation that started the movement. Learn how to collaborate with your digital partner—with clarity and humanity.
- **FOCUS BOT**
  Reclaim Your Attention in an Age of Distraction
  Practical tools for clarity, flow, and balance in a fragmented world.
- **CREATIVE BOT**
  How to Be an Artist in the Age of ChatGPT
  Use ChatGPT to unlock your creative flow.
- **CASH BOT**
  Reframe Your Relationship with Money
  Build a mindset of abundance and learn to create, save, and spend with intention.

- **CALM BOT**
  How to Stay Steady When the World Shakes
  Learn to quiet the noise, regulate your thoughts, and use your chatbot as a calm companion in an age of anxiety.

Follow Sugar Gay Isber McMillan

Instagram: **@SugarGayIsber**
Amazon Author Page:
amazon.com/author/sugargayisbermcmillan
Website: **TheWOWBookCo.com**
For media, collaborations, or podcast invitations, visit **GayIsber.com**

Support Independent Publishing

Every review matters. If you enjoyed *Calm Bot*, we would appreciate it if you could share your thoughts on Amazon or Goodreads.

Your words help more readers discover the *Talk*

to Your Tools™ series and support the growth of independent creators.

Thank you for reading my book.

Scan to see all books by Sugar Gay Isber McMillan

"When I started talking to my Bot, I found my world got quieter and my future looked brighter."
— Reader Review

SUGAR GAY ISBER

ART, BOOKS & JEWELS

The WOW Book Co.

Sugar Gay Isber McMillan

Sugar

Made in the USA
Coppell, TX
05 November 2026

11301607R00063